SUCCESS OR FAILURE

IN

YOUR RELATIONSHIP

Four Basic Principles Needed
IF
You Want a Lifetime Partner

By

K.E. Martin

D1593682

800-582-4178
info@JonRosePublishing.com

SUCCESS OR FAILURE

IN

YOUR RELATIONSHIP

by

K.E. Martin

ISBN-13: 978-1-63089-016-2

INTRODUCTION

Have you ever wondered what it takes to have a good relationship? Are you someone who wants a healthy relationship but doesn't know how to go about it? Or are you already in a relationship, but you're uncertain if it's with the right person? I've known of many people who were in a relationship or married suddenly break-up or get a divorce. For whatever reason, the relationship simply broke down. These people come from all walks of life; it happens to men, women, young, and old. Many of us—well, *most* of us—have beliefs that guide us. Our beliefs may not work well in a relationship, but they do guide us.

People are experts in all kinds of things, from construction to management, from design to engineering, from line assembly to mass production, from waitressing to cooking, from groundskeeping to farming, from motivational speaking to self-help, from housekeeping to running a successful company or corporation. People can give us all kinds of guidance for personal and business relations and success. I once heard author and motivational speaker Tony Robbins talk about drug abuse; he has seen all kinds of people, from the poor to the corporate executive, have substance abuse issues and seek his help. Many will give you all kinds of guidance, but they will also say, "Just don't ask me about relationships. I just got divorced, and I'm no expert on the subject, but I can tell you about (whatever their subject matter is)." Or you might get something like, "We got married quickly, but after 6 or 7 years, I couldn't take him not helping around the house, or making me do all the cooking; it just wasn't fair. Now my new guy is nothing like that; even after work, he still takes care of me."

Every relationship is different. We all have different expectations. Many people make the right decisions when it comes to a partner; many people make the wrong decisions. When someone picks a partner, it is often based on just a few ingredients of the required mix. People never think of the entire mix and make sure all the ingredients are there. This is human nature. Do we really think our relationships out well? Many times, we think we do, but as time moves on, and as we change, so does the relationship. Will your current relationship still work in the future, or are you just living in the now? This is a book to help you decide if you've found your true love. I'm not going to tell you how to date or give you pick-up lines. I'm going to explain to you how to know if the person you're with is the right person for you. I'm going to explain how to know if you're truly happy with your significant other, or if it's just wishful thinking. This is a book you need when you want to know if something is missing, or if you've found the right person.

You might be wondering, "How does this guy possibly know what it takes?" Well, after 20 years of marriage with the wrong woman, I've had a long time to figure out why I made such a mistake in my life. It had nothing to do with having kids, as we both agreed to start a family. It had more to do with a relationship that was not fulfilling. I've spent countless hours researching the subject of relationships and relating to my own failures. Although my wife and I certainly had many good times, in the long run, my marriage turned out not to be sustainable. I'm not talking about the marriage just going sour; I'm talking about a disconnect between two people. She and I got along for many years, or so I thought, but there was always something missing. Maybe it was expectation, but as time went on, I looked at what was wrong and at what was missing. It took me some time to realize where I had failed, but I have come up with the reasons why. I now understand where I went wrong. What to do about it is another matter. What do you do when you're in an unhappy relationship? That becomes a matter of personal choice and (I dare say) affordability. So that is a topic for another time. The topic for now is, how do you know when you've found the right person? There are four ingredients that will help you determine if the person you are with is right for you, and if you will be happy in this relationship. So my friends, read on and absorb what I have written. It will help anyone who wants a long-term relationship to understand the mix that is needed if you want it to last. There are no excesses or guarantees in this life, but I will cover straightforward topics that every relationship needs if it is to survive the test of time.

THE FOUR PRINCIPLES

I

PERSONALITIES

1. Personalities

i. I will start off with the first principle, because it isn't a hard one to figure out. Most people will come to this conclusion subconsciously when meeting someone. Most of us will know whether we like someone and want to get to know him/ her better. This does not mean a relationship will start, but it is helpful to know that the person you are interested in seems compatible with you. Personality alone is not enough; you need the other three ingredients, but it is a good starting point. When personalities mesh well together and when two people have an attraction to one another, that's a very good sign. But you need to pay attention and not just let sudden excitement get to you.

- Personalities have to mesh well under many circumstances, not just in good times; they have to work in the not-so-good times. You don't really know a person until the chips are down; you need to face bad times together to gauge your true compatibility. Life may get very rough (there could be a number of different reasons for this), and the two of you may totally disagree on how to move forward. Suddenly resources that you are both used to might no longer be there, and you have to go without. When your partner is with you during the bad times, and they are understanding and helpful, then you have a solid foundation to be a long-lasting couple. If your partner is using the blame game and isn't very understanding or tolerable of you, that's a good indicator that you're in an unhealthy relationship. I'm not saying people don't disagree; we all do from time to time. But when the arguments occur all the time, often daily, then that's not a healthy relationship. Disagreements are human nature, but they should not be part of your everyday life. I've seen couples continuously argue. Sometimes, it's almost humorous the way they go at each other; other times, it's very unhealthy and sometimes dangerous for one of them. You need to take a good hard look at the situation and see if that person is truly the right one for you. Many times, the situation will be well beyond anyone's control.

a. Here is an example of this: In California and in New York, parents' civil liberties were taken away with mandatory vaccinations for all school-aged children. This was a constitutional infringement that was totally uncalled for; it was politically-driven, though everyone was told it was for the greater good. As parents, you have no control over that. As a couple, you can be at opposite sides of the issue, as many parents are. This is where the two of you need to talk and decide what is best. I can tell you if you remain on opposite sides, then your child or children will be the ones who suffer.

b. I will add, the same issue almost happened in New Jersey, but concerned parents gathered in protest at the state house and successfully defeated it (3 times to date). It is on the table in Connecticut (as well as several other states). An issue like this is very deep, and possibly very dangerous for children (those who are immune compromised and can't handle the vaccine schedule, which is about 30% of all children, will be vaccine injured). Parents will very often disagree on this subject matter; those who follow the CDC will be for it, but those that don't follow them will be against it. It really comes down to a personal choice, but it is one that needs to be made. The way the two of you handle it will have repercussions in your relationship.

In those cases, educating both of you is the best course of action. Whom do you listen to? Why do you listen to that source? This is a point, often critical, for your next step in life. Never discount such a crucial step. It has often been said, "If I only knew the information that I know now, I would have made a completely different decision. Nobody told me the truth. I believed the professionals, or those I thought were professional, but they all gave me bad advice." There are all kinds of reasons for this, but it can be life-changing. Always proceed with getting proper knowledge before you make such a potential life-changing decision.

- Whatever the situation may arise, you always need to get the facts first, especially if the decision could potentially change your future. A lifetime of arguing is not the best for anyone to live with.

- Ego will get in the way. A partner who has the idea that the other is always wrong, or that they should never give into the other, is someone who cannot be satisfied. That is a situation that will not be healthy for either of you. The purpose of having a relationship is to enjoy life together, not satisfy the ego of another. Two personalities that are alpha male (a female can have an alpha male personality too) are not going to do very well together. One will learn to give into the other, or it will be a constant clash.

- Another item I can add deals with the perfectionist. This is when one partner is not satisfied with the way another partner does things; it could be anything. For whatever reason, one partner sees something not being done right. A lot of us get bothered because we see something done wrong, and we know we can fix it; I'm not talking about that. An example would be the relationship with me and my wife. I can cook to a degree, and she lets me do some simple stuff, but for the most part, I will never cook to her liking. I'm not terrible at it, but I'm not very good at it either. Unfortunately, she is so particular about it that I cannot cook anything to her satisfaction. So, no matter what the event, she does the cooking. The only time she has any relief is when her mother comes to see the grandkids (usually once a week) and cooks for us. Even though my wife will still find something to complain about (such as the kitchen setup, or things not being put back in the right place), at least she's able to get a little relief. If I cook, forget about it. I learned a long time ago, the only way to satisfy a perfectionist is to let that person do the task him/herself. There is no way to satisfy such a personality. Only another perfectionist would have a chance at satisfying the like-minded.

• My father had several relationships after he left my mother. He was compatible with these women, but another ingredient caused each relationship to fail. There were at least two women (at separate times) that he would have married. I say that because I always told him he would meet the right woman. His comment was always, "Well, I've met her twice, arguably three times already," which was true. This led me to think and realize what was missing. Now I'll get into that later in the book, but it's very important to understand that all four principles (ingredients) are needed if you are seeking to find a lifetime partner.

- My older brother has been married several times. His first marriage was definitely a personality mismatch. They were young, and it seemed like a good idea at the time. That marriage gave him his only child. So in that sense, it worked out well. But the two of them just were not a match and had completely different personalities. This is one of the fates of the young: you think you're in love, only to find out sometime afterwards, you don't agree on a lot of things. A personality clash becomes very evident.

- Unfortunately for him, he had a personality clash with his second wife as well. He thought it was a good idea at the time, but another union wasn't meant to be. It was one of those situations where mental disagreement, or I could say mental abuse, was part of the issue. I could also say that with my own marriage. My wife is wired differently than me. She does not know how to get to the point. She always asks me questions to trap me instead of telling me what the issue is. So, we get mad at each other all the time. If it were just the two of us, that would be one thing, but we have two children, and she always has an attitude in front of them. I have never agreed with expressing oneself like that in front of children, but I've never been able to stop her from doing so. In her case, it's an ego thing; she loves to prove me wrong. She has our daughter convinced that Mommy is always right, and Daddy is always wrong. When I come home from work, it would be nice to get a rundown of the day's events, to know what's going on, if anything, but nope. If I don't ask, she will barely say anything. She will always find a reason to delay explanation just so she can get mad at me when I don't do what she wants. Of course, it would be nice of her to tell me upfront, but that would be too easy. She is terrible at explaining anything to me. So, we live with a constant disconnect.

ii. It's often said that opposites attract. Personalities can be the same or opposite, but they must comingle and be a good fit. If personalities are in constant conflict, then the relationship might not be a good one. Sure, it's okay to have disagreements and differences of opinion, but conflict is what will get in the way of a good relationship. This goes deeper than just personalities, as I'll explain in later points, but conflict is one aspect that will get in the way.

iii. Another point is when one does not want to talk to the other. If one partner is busy with a topic and doesn't want the other partner to interfere, that's okay, but when conversation gets stale, and when it's a burden to talk to the other partner, that's not good. Personalities have to be such where both partners enjoy the conversation and company of the other. People need to work to survive, but your partner is your priority. If you get to the point where you prefer time away from your partner all the time, then you're headed down the wrong path. Your relationship is not doing well. You and your partner will need space from each other at times, but you should always want to come back to each other. The most loving relationship is the one where the two of you simply want each other, when you both feel it's much better to be together than to be separate, and when you enjoy spending time together. The lack of this does not make for a healthy relationships.

2. Toxic relationships

i. Too many people are in relationships that are simply unhealthy. They have an excuse for staying together, but one or both parties are miserable. I've seen this many, many times. One or both of them simply feels stuck, and they have no idea what to do about it. When you realize you are in a toxic relationship, you need to get out. Life is not meant to be a struggle that you are going through. Life is meant to be enjoyable. Many people are struggling right now in their relationships, but life is meant to be enjoyed. If you are not happy in your relationship, then you should not be in it. Sure, you do not know what to do many times. Maybe you cannot afford to leave; it's just too expensive, and you have too many obligations. There is always an excuse that prevents you from moving on and enjoying life. I've seen this time and time again. For many, it seems there is no light at the end of the tunnel, but you need to pay attention to your circumstance. You need to believe that life will get better. The universe is actually working in your favor. It may not seem like it at all, but believe me, as long as your belief is firm, as long as deep in your subconscious you know life will improve, then events will start to take place that will be of great benefit to you.

- I actually saw this with my own sister. She and her first husband seemed very happy. They started having kids. My sister was a waitress at the time. Sometime after their first daughter was born, within the first year, she called me and needed a ride to work. I went to pick her up, and I saw her husband, my brother-in-law, driving away on his motorcycle. I didn't think much of it, so I continued to her house. She was standing outside holding her daughter. I asked if she was ready. "No," was the answer. It turns out, her husband wanted to go to a party instead of staying home and watching his daughter while my sister, his wife, was trying to make a living. She had to call in sick to work at about the time she was supposed to be there. Unfortunately, I can tell you many more stories like that. They actually had two more children over the years, but life was a constant struggle for her. Their relationship was up and down – more down actually. It took her about 13 years to finally leave him. It was a relationship she wished she didn't have, but she needed to be able to provide for her children without him before she could end the marriage. In the long run, it did work out for her, but a good chunk of her life was spent in turmoil. A positive note from it is that all three of her children came out just fine. My sister had issues with her oldest child for some time, because of the influence of the father, and she had to keep all private information locked-up, but her second husband put up with it. Yes, a toxic relationship can reach beyond the first marriage and interfere with future relationships. So you want to be cautious about staying in such a situation.

3. Likes, dislikes, attitudes

i. In the best relationships, both of you have the same likes and dislikes. It's best when you complement one another. This doesn't happen all the time, but most of the time, a couple can get through minor differences without giving it much thought. Sometimes it's more difficult, as I've seen many couples argue. Well, just about every couple can argue, but some have nice blowouts. Many times, it comes down to one of you having an attitude. When one of you is like that, then the other has the choice to submit or challenge. I've done it myself, many times. Most of the time, I will not give into a bad attitude, no matter what. If my wife has a bad attitude, that's her problem. Of course, that can just escalate tensions, as it almost always does, but many people will say, "I'm not submissive," and they will not back down. This will just add to more tension within a relationship. That's why personalities and attitudes are important to think about if you want a long-term or lifetime relationship. If you compromise, be careful. You don't want to make a decision you'll regret years down the road. There is nothing wrong with minor compromise, but when one partner compromises too much, they end up regretting their decision years later. So carefully decide if it is a reasonable compromise.

- Referring to my sister's first relationship again, I know if I had been in her shoes and my spouse wanted to go to a party instead of watch our first child while I had to go to work, I probably would have ended the relationship then and there. I would have suffered with the consequences for the short term, and made plans for a long-term goal without that inconsiderate spouse of mine. Luckily, my sister is not like me because they went on to have two more children. It would be years later that she would finally break up with him.

4. How well do two people communicate?

i. Many couples fail at this. One person is just wired differently than the other. I've been dealing with this for over 20 years; it never gets better. When you are wired differently than your partner, you end up with two people who don't communicate well and who will have serious differences. Sometimes, it can work out, as I've seen, but that is usually when attitudes don't interfere. What you need to look at is every piece and see if there is enough to keep the relationship on solid ground. Every relationship has give and take, but it has to be mutually satisfying for both; otherwise, regret will be very apparent.

- Lack of good communication combined with attitude is what I face every day. If the communication were there, then our relationship might be a bit easier. I'm not saying I'm a great guy, but I am a hard worker. I've been working my entire life, and I only wish that could be appreciated, but it isn't. My wife and I have a continued communication gap. It's apparent that our personalities don't match up very well. I like openness and explanation.

She likes openness as well, but explanation is like pulling teeth, and it's always with an attitude. So, that tells you how life can be.

- An example of this is when we went to her former place of employment after our son was born (she had worked in NYC). The building had a revolving door. She said, "Wait here," as she went through the door, then I started to proceed. What she did not tell me was that there was a side door. She had to go through the revolving door, go to the side door and open it. She didn't have the courtesy to even point me to the side door from the beginning. I didn't see it, nor did I have a clue it was there. She ended up shouting at me, "Are you crazy! Bla, bla, bla, bla...." I should have thought it through myself, but I didn't think of it, and she certainly did not communicate anything to me. Had the situation been reversed, I would have pointed her to the side door from the beginning, realizing that she probably wouldn't even know about it. This is the type of non-communication that wears a relationship down after many years.

5. Expectation

i. Part of personality has to deal with expectation. How often do you automatically expect something or a situation to go a certain way, but then it doesn't? This is a real indicator that the two of you are not on the same page. When your expectations are not met, for whatever reason, it becomes disappointing. It's usually not the end of the world, but it can play a role in how you understand your relationship should be going. If your expectations are consistently not being met, then you're not going to be in the best of moods. It won't be enough to break a relationship, at least not at first; plus, you will need other ingredients that are also not working in your favor. So, just keep this in mind.

• My expectation with communication proved to be a fantasy. I'm used to open communication and good explanation. I mainly had that type of open communication with friends and even in business relations, but when it came to my marriage, expectations were often proven wrong. An example of this is when we had our first and second children. After each birth, my mother spent one week with us to help out. My mom basically had to be referee. My wife would say one thing, or I would say one thing, and neither one of us understood the other to the proper degree, so my mother would interpret for both of us. She actually completed the thought that one of us was trying to express. The added benefit to this was that my wife would always get an attitude during conversation, so with my mother acting as referee, it kept my wife in check. Life for those separate weeks went much smoother that way.

II

MENTAL STIMULATION

1. Do you and your partner talk about views and interests?

i. Viewpoints are only one point of interest. Two people don't have to agree, but each should have a good reason for their specific view on an issue. When an argument sets in, it's because one partner cannot express a viewpoint that makes sense to the other. It's okay to disagree, but realize that two people can and often do think differently. Arguably, the breakdown in communication happens when one person refuses to be open-minded. Lack of openness with one's opinion leads to conflict—that's just human nature. Our society has bred close-minded individuals who have very little to no empathy. This has caused many couples to grow apart. "Well, that's not the way I was raised." One spouse simply refuses to understand the other's point of view. This is also called being stubborn. Sometimes, it's okay; many times, it's not and can lead to a breakup.

- I've seen where the dominant person in the relationship or marriage ridicules the other. Sometimes it's done in public. Most of the time, it happens in private. This is where one person is simply caught in a bad relationship and feels stuck. Too often, a partner ends up saying, "Are you trying to make me feel stupid?" Mental stimulation is absent and has been replaced with mental abuse. When this happens, the relationship has no real cure. One partner simply feels stuck, and they need to figure out how to leave.

- Another example is when one partner never believes the other partner. For whatever reason, one partner thinks the other is always holding something back. One time, I had to explain to my brother's second wife how I met the woman I was going to marry. It was actually a surprise to the entire family at the time because I had been a bachelor, and no one knew I was even dating, let alone in a serious relationship with a woman. Then all of a sudden, I was getting married. Well, my brother's second wife didn't believe her husband, my brother, had known nothing about this relationship I was in, not until I explained to her the situation. Ironically, they broke up one week after I got married. For them, it was not a good marriage from the start. There was a personality mismatch, plus a mental stimulation mismatch. It just was not going to work for them in the long term.

2. This is not personalities but rather stimulating conversation.

i. When there is enticing conversation, it doesn't matter if two people even like each other or not (of course, it always helps), but when conversation on something mutually interesting is involved, it has a way of being pleasurable to the mind. So many couples lack this simple but very important principal. Very often, one partner has a mindset in one direction, while the other partner is trying but not getting anywhere. This happens a lot in families where parents simply grow apart. The conversation is no longer there. The enjoyment of conversation has left them. It is now a struggle to communicate in an effective manner. This in some part can spell doom for a relationship. What often happens is one or both partners ignore the obvious. They simply let it go, hoping things will get better. Will they? Sometimes yes, but many times no. It's far too important to make sure that this step is not ignored during your relationship. Personalities are needed, but without the right mental stimulation, where do you think the relationship will go? Trust me, it will not go to a good place. Too often, if a couple wants to stay together, then compromise is due, but even compromise will have its limits. One partner will end up resenting the relationship, often with the feeling that it's becoming one-sided. Be very careful with this principal, and don't take it for granted that the situation will improve. Life is meant to be a joy with your partner, not a burden. If it doesn't feel right, then take a look at yourself. Is it you or some outside influence that you might or might not be able to control? You need to understand what both of you expect. When your conversations are natural and easy flowing, then you have something. If they are boring and drawn-out, then you don't really have the best relationship. Happiness is a two-way street. Personalities and mental stimulation may be closely related, but there are differences that need to be understood.

- My father had a PhD, while my mother got her GED after raising a family. He was a college professor. There was no mental stimulation for him. His topics of discussion were of no interest to my mother. While it was fun and a lot of work to have kids and raise a family, by the time we were all in school, he was having issues with the intellectual difference. At one point, he would take my older brother and myself to the college gym every Friday night. A bunch of fellow professors would play a few rounds of basketball. It seemed to be their release for the week. I later found out from him that he used to live for that; he needed to get away. We almost bought land in another state; we went there once a month or so on the weekends. We discussed the possibility of him working during the week and coming home on the weekends because of the long drive. It was just his way of looking for

26

some way to cope with his marriage. At the time, my mother had no idea there was an issue, but my father was having lots of trouble handling his marriage. In later years, when we would talk about past events and times, she made the comment, "He was always running somewhere." It seems that was what he needed at the time, until he met someone, which would become his first girlfriend, and he finally left my mother. She was of course shocked by this, but he couldn't handle it anymore.

- With me and my wife, even though we have a severe disconnect in communication, she is good about topics for discussion. It's odd that her personality is such where we don't have general conversation to explain everyday events, but when it comes to topics that can have an impact on us, she researches it a lot (though she doesn't clean the house very much). After her research, she talks to me about events that could have an impact on us. This type of mental stimulation is fine. Unfortunately for us, it's the only one out of the four principles needed for a lasting relationship. We fall short on the other three.

- I also have to add that I can be a little slow and not comprehend or understand people that well. This drives my wife nuts. She has trouble with my lack of understanding. When my mother used to come visit, she often served as referee (as I mentioned previously), so that helped the situation. But my wife gets frustrated with me often; either I don't understand what she's asking, or she doesn't know how to explain it to me. No matter which way it is, mental frustration sets in quickly. At times, the explanation comes out; other times, an argument commences. This is where the level of communication directly effects the mental attitude.

III

SEXUAL SATISFACTION

1. Physical attraction

i. Physical attraction is part of any real relationship. Whenever we look at someone, the attraction factor is on most people's minds. For those who are satisfied in a relationship, they may not gauge this as much as others, but most people look at someone and quickly determine how attractive they are. "Beauty is in the eye of the beholder" is an age-old cliché that is very to the point.

- Combined with other factors, physical attraction can be very good, but it can also interfere with a relationship. Many times, one partner is no longer attracted to the other partner. One partner turns cold to the other partner. One partner doesn't get turned on any longer. What is it? Why does this happen? Whatever caused the attraction is now gone. One partner just doesn't feel like having sex; in this case, it's now the lack of attraction that is the cause (more on this in a moment).

2. Intimacy

i. We are creatures who need some form of companionship. In a real relationship, sex is very normal. Sex was made to be pleasurable. Don't be worried about it, but rather, always enjoy it. It's often the greatest form of love that two people can have with one another. It's not meant to be hidden. Open affection for the one you love should be very natural.

- Sadly, we never see this. Society leaves intimacy in the home. Very rarely is any form of subtle intimacy seen outside. It's just the way it's viewed. Sure, sometimes people, especially teens, can be seen holding hands or walking arm in arm, but not so much with adults. It's just my observation. Many of you may disagree, but it's what I see.

3. A natural need for affection

i. Many of us have a strong need for affection. We need the love and attention of another. We like to hold hands and put our arm around someone. We like to be playful with that special someone. It's all very natural, and there's no need to be shy about it. It's okay to show simple gestures of affection for the one you love.

- Nothing beats true love. When you have found your lifetime partner, there is no better feeling in the world. One of the ways you can tell is when you both have the need for affection, and it just won't die out. Yup, even later in life, when you both still have that need for affection, nothing beats it.

4. Sexual frustration

i. If one partner craves sex and the other partner is not interested, this alone can drive a couple apart. Why does this happen? Hormonal issues can interfere with sex drive. As stated previously, it's very often that one partner is no longer attracted to the other partner. There is usually nothing that will fix this. When two people grow apart, it's time to move on. It may never be the best time, but when one partner is frustrated, and the other partner shows no interest, it's time to end the relationship. Yes, it sounds blunt, but the other choice is to remain in an unhappy relationship, one that you will grow to resent. This is one reason why so many married people cheat. They are stuck in a relationship that provides for them, but they are very unsatisfied in it. The easy way is to find someone on the side in the same situation. Meet up when you can, and each of you gets your sexual frustrations out. It happens a lot. There's nothing wrong with it, but in this situation, you may want to see if you can arrange to leave your spouse. Timing could be an issue, but you will never be satisfied in your current marriage.

- Many couples stick it out, especially after spending a good part of their lives together, but the happiness is now gone. The marriage is just for convenience at this point. It is convenient because it would be very hard to actually separate. The cost of separation can be a factor that keeps couples stuck in their situation. Lots of couples fall into this scenario; they simply can't afford to divorce so they stick it out. One or both of them may cheat, but that is the only option they see.

- Other times it's just age. When a couple gets old, it's not possible for them to change. They may like each other, they may even still love each other, but they also have to put up with each other. There are so many reasons why a relationship gets stuck like this. I would say by the time you are elderly, then your options have greatly diminished. I don't often see an elderly couple separate, as it's much easier to ride it out till the end of your days. Although when one partner dies, the surviving partner will often look for someone for companionship. This is very normal and welcome. One never wants to be elderly and alone. It will happen to many of us, but to find someone or to be in a home with others is the preferred choice.

ii. There can also be a couple of different physical conditions as to why a woman cannot enjoy being with her partner. (I will preface this by saying I'm not a doctor, nor can I give medical advice, but I will still share my knowledge with you.)

- A yeast infection is very common for a woman at some time in her life. "Also called vaginal candidiasis, vaginal yeast infection affects up to 3 out of 4 women at some point in their lifetimes. Many women experience at least two episodes" (Mayo Clinic). This can prevent a woman from enjoying sex.

- Another such condition that might prevent a woman from enjoying intercourse is bad gut flora, such as Candida or Clostridium (there are more of them). Gut flora is something we all need, but it is most important to have more good flora than bad flora. Think of it this way, we all have good soldiers in our GI track that help us digest food and keep bad soldiers in check. We usually have about 95% good soldiers to about 5% bad soldiers. There are many people who have an overabundance of bad soldiers; they override the good soldiers. One way to tell that someone has an overabundance of bad soldiers is when someone has a degree of white foam in their mouth; that's a good indicator of Candida or Clostridium overload in the body. When this happens, we need to kill off the bad soldiers. With an improper balance of gut flora, loads of bad things can happen to us, including many aliments that we just can't figure out the cause. (On a side note, many babies and children can have such a condition, which can lead to things such as gluten intolerance and autism.) If a woman has an overabundance of bad flora, it could impede her sexual desire and performance.

- There is another condition that prevents a woman from wanting sexual intercourse. It's called vulvodynia. The definition of vulvodynia is "chronic pain in the vulva, the area on the outside of a woman's genitals" (Cleveland Clinic). The cause is unknown to doctors. It could be the result of "sexual assault, injury to or irritation of the nerves surrounding your vulvar region, past vaginal infections, allergies or sensitive skin" (Mayo Clinic). If this is the case, then the partner needs to be very understanding. Both the Mayo Clinic and the Cleveland Clinic (among many others) discuss this condition and possible ways to help a woman eliminate the pain.

iii. Let's not forget about the guys

- Yes, there is erectile dysfunction. Now again, I'm not a doctor, nor can I give any medical advice. Many males need to see their primary care doctor for a treatment plan. But what I can do is give several suggestions that can certainly help. I started to study health and nutrition way back in the 1980s. Through time, I learned several healthy dietary habits. I don't always stick to it, but I have certainly improved my own health at certain times in my life. One thing to point out – and it's no real secret – is don't eat too much starch. Many of us love pasta and rice, potatoes and bread and sugars; these are all simple carbs that will undermine your health and sexual performance. There isn't much nutritional value in them. Complex carbs are what we should be eating. I learned a long time ago that a person should eat to support their blood and immune system. This is done by eating good vegetables, healthy meats, and healthy fat (small amount) with every meal. Dr. Barry Sears explains this wonderfully in his book *The Omega RX Zone.* I would encourage everyone who is nutrition conscience to read it. That book taught me about proper diet and omega 3 fish oil and its importance to help control internal inflammation.

a. What is internal inflammation? Traditional medicine should be all over this, but they usually are not. Internal inflammation is what will cause you to have a heart attack or stroke. It will also interfere with males and their ability to perform sexually. A simple blood test that everyone should request when you get blood work done will tell you what your internal inflammation level is; it's call C-reactive protein. It's nothing new; your doctor or cardiologist should be well aware of it and test it automatically, but they don't. You need to ask for it. You need to ask them to check your C-reactive protein (it may be called HR-CRP, or something like that) and your vitamin D level. These are simple tests that they never do. Your C-reactive protein should be about 1.5. This number can be hard to reach, as many people are often as high as 2.5. If your level is 3.5 or higher, then your internal inflammation is indicating that you're in a heart attack or stroke range. This is where someone will have a sudden heart attack and will have no idea why it happened.

b. I will also add that there are several good sources for fish oil supplementation. Dr. Barry Sears sells one of the best brands on the market, but it is very pricey. Nordic Naturals is another good brand, as are Carlson's and Green Pasture, but they are all pricey.

c. I just mentioned Vitamin D as well. Most people are deficient in this vitamin and need supplementation to get their blood level high enough to better support their immune system. Vitamin D3 supplementation along with vitamin K2 (for absorption) is great for your immune system. Most doctors get their vitamin D3 from Biotech Pharmacal, as it has very little additives; 5,000 IU is optimum, but have your blood work done to ensure you're in the proper range. Vitamin K2 (the MK-7 version) is actually much more expensive, but because of the absorption, it's well worth it; 100 mcg works well.

d. I'm going to tell you about another supplement that also helps control internal inflammation: vitamin E. This is not a store-bought version, but rather a full-spectrum vitamin E. The best one that I know of and take myself is from the A.C. Grace Company, and it's called Unique E. There are some people who won't be able to tolerate it, as too much can be toxic for their system, while many others can take larger doses of it and benefit from daily use. So, you have to see what your system can tolerate.

e. By taking control of your nutrition in this fashion, you could see an improvement in your sexual performance. Now again, I'm not a doctor, nor can I give medical advice. I do know that through proper nutrition, along with taking these supplements, there will be a very good benefit for the body and immune system.

f. Get your blood flowing. Exercise when possible. At least take a good walk. We are not meant to have a sedentary life. We all need movement; some form of physical exercise is required for everyone.

g. Get outside whenever possible. We have a couple of parks by us. On the weekends, we like to go to the park, have some snacks, then take a good walk. Doing something like this a few times a week is a great idea. You know your schedule, so try to adjust whenever you can.

h. Don't fall for the "small amount of daily

alcohol is good for you." Alcohol is toxic to the liver. The resveratrol in wine can be beneficial, but alcohol itself has no benefit.

IV

FINANCIAL SECURITY

1. Don't let anyone fool you; finances will always have an impact on a relationship.

i.   There are many times when two people agree to work for a living and have a family. There are many times when a couple realizes they are average Americans, or their standard of living is just going to be average. There is nothing wrong with that, as most people will fall into this category. What I'm bringing up here is when one partner has to carry the burden for the family without much help from the other partner. I've seen this many times where it's just a continuous life struggle. Eventually, one partner will get so frustrated with the relationship that they start looking for a way out. Sometimes, it may take years, but they will not be a happy couple. I will further say that most of the time, the relationship will not work out. There will always be an exception, but finances do interfere with happiness.

- I have to refer back to my sister, which I brought up in the personalities/toxic relationship section. Finances were always an issue in her marriage. When she realized she couldn't rely on her husband to bring in enough money, or to even be steadily employed, she started to sponge off the family. My father took the brunt of it, as he subsidized her income, though unwillingly, for some time. They went to each family member during the course of the marriage for financial help. I had heard some of the stories from my father and older brother, so when my sister came to me, I foolishly lent her one of my credit lines. Unfortunately, this did not make my brother-in-law personally responsible to pay back what he was borrowing. They simply couldn't make it on their own. Over the course of the next couple of years, my sister would always come to me to borrow money so she could pay bills. Finally at one point, when she was trying to break-up with him, she came to my house, asking for a good amount of money, but I turned her down. Just 5 weeks later, her husband went on vacation. She was trying to pay bills, and he went on a vacation! I was so glad I didn't give in to her requests and give her money that time. Apparently, she kept sponging from the family, but he was not aware. This was a big mistake my family made. None of us should have ever helped her out. I'll explain more in a moment. But first, I'll tell you, just before she was finally able to leave him, they had to live with my mother. My mother reluctantly took them in (which was also a mistake), so they could save up to get their own place. They were there for well over a year, and it was driving my mother nuts. One day, she came home, and the kids were alone. When my sister got home, mother asked her what happened. My brother-in-law had gone on his yearly vacation to California. WHAT? My mother blew her top. Here they were, supposedly saving to get their own apartment, and he went on vacation. My mother put all his things on the front lawn; he was never allowed to step foot in her house again. My mother saw what a bad husband and father he was, always wanting to go out and party and never wanting to stay with the family. Forget about working for a living—he wasn't interested.

- At one point, years earlier, he stayed with me for several weeks. He had mentioned he had no interest in working. That's when I also learned he had no idea what his finances were. All he knew was my sister paid the bills. This is why I said it was a mistake for the family to help her out. Her husband wasn't a responsible person. He did not provide financial support for his family, and they ended up having three children! My sister kept coming to her family for financial support. In hindsight, none of us should have helped her, as we were a crutch. She needed to learn how to survive on her own. If that meant getting government assistance (which she actually did for a short time), then that's what she needed to do. Our family continuously helping her, while her husband had no idea, was completely wrong. He had no incentive to find any real work as long as she could somehow pay the bills. That was a mistake that would be corrected after about ten years of assistance from us, her family. When she was finally able to leave my mother's house and get her own apartment without him, she was able to do it because she was working two jobs. We had all cut her off; she was not with her husband any longer (which was a relief), and she was able to pay her bills. She would actually meet the man who would be her second husband shortly, but that's a completely different story.

2. A working-class couple will be okay many times.

i.   This is the case for the working class. We make a living, some better, some worse, but we all work and make a living. I will never put anyone down for doing a job and making an honest living. Whatever you do, it's fine for you. All working-class couples fall into this category. We all work and provide for our family. This is life as we know it. There is nothing wrong with making an honest living. We are actually the backbone of the American economy. There is over 100 million of us working-class families who support local business with our dollars being spent. We need goods and services to survive. The more we can supply to ourselves, the better our individual lives are. Of course, we can always use more. Heck, many of us would love to win the lottery, but we all manage by working for a living. As long as we make a decent living, and properly budget, then we will keep a roof over our heads and food on the table.

ii. What will break-up most of us is one of the other categories. Maybe the level of sex isn't cutting it for one spouse, or the mental stimulation simply isn't there. As I mentioned earlier about my own parents, my father was a PhD, while my mother got her GED after having a family. There was no mental stimulation for him. His topics of discussion were of no interest to my mother. Sex was never a problem, as I was told, but finances were difficult. My mother would have stayed with him no matter what, but my father could not tolerate the relationship after 15 years. He had other relationships, but finances were always the problem. As I mentioned previously, he worked for a living, he was a college professor, but they only make so much money. So, he had a string of girlfriends for a number of years. Each would move on after a period of time. One of the 4 principles was always missing. Love alone, or what some people think is love, often doesn't have much to do with it. When you're older, family has a lot to do with it. When my father did eventually meet someone who would become his future wife, his family was in the way. So, he changed his life. Now, sometimes that is for the good; sometimes it's not. That will be an individual or family decision. But never discount the financial factor in any situation. That is the worst thing you can do.

- I mentioned in the personalities section that my father had met 2 or 3 women he would have married, but each of them eventually moved on. Finances were the issue. He would tell me he had nothing to offer. The women in his circle expected a certain quality of life. He had a family and always lived beyond his means. He had no real success to offer anyone. The first woman he dated (the woman he left my mother for) was with him for several years. After she got her law degree, that basically ended the relationship. His finances proved to be a deciding factor. The personalities were good, as well as mental stimulation. I'm guessing sex was fine, but you need all four ingredients to be agreed upon if it's going to work.

- His second girlfriend seemed like a very good fit. Maybe family had something to do with it, but again, finances were the key. He had met two good women who eventually moved on because of finances. There was a third woman who was younger with a pleasant personality. They got along very well, but he told me again, he had nothing to offer. He just made a living. Several years later, I met her again. She was pleasant and talkative, but by this time, she was married. She was still friends with my father, and I'm sure that if he'd had more confidence in himself, he could have pushed the relationship further, but then again, I don't know what her expectations were. Just the way he said he had nothing to offer indicated to me that she had a certain level of expectation in her life. Her husband did bear a resemblance to my father, but I'm guessing he didn't have a premade family for her. Now we were all adults by then, so my father could have simply moved on without us, but that didn't happen at that point in his life. The two of them were still friendly to each other, and that was about it.

- When he did finally get remarried (which ended up being years later), his new wife's expectations were much lower. She basically needed someone to live off of, and for what-ever reason, he was willing to be the one. The family never understood the relationship. She was not in the best state of mind. In fact, her mental state was a problem for all of us. At the time he met her, his mother was still alive. My father basically dumped the entire family for this woman. He not only ignored his four children, but he even stopped taking the four-hour drive to see his own mother.

She was very elderly at the time and was very upset at this. He used to go see her at least twice a year, but then he stopped going entirely. At one point, he took a trip to see his older brother. I'm not sure what happened, but my father was told his wife wasn't allowed there any longer. My uncle was a very passive guy. I met him several times in my life. To get him upset, she must have had to be a total pain in the neck, at least beyond what is tolerable for most people. My uncle had seven children, so patience is one thing he had. There was some big disconnect, or he caught on to her act very quickly.

- A couple of friends of mine were together for a very long time. We were neighbors growing up, so we had known each other since childhood. He dated his girlfriend for 17 years before they finally got married. His father was always a worker. He always worked as well. He did not go to college, so his income was limited. Her parents lived in an apartment complex. Her father was in real estate. I talked to him on occasion. He was a smart guy, but he wasn't successful and could barely afford the apartment for his family. So, her background was financially less than his. They were a good couple. She was always eager to get married. In their case, they were both broke. They made a living. He always worked and provided the best he could. Their situation was fine for both of them. When you come from a meager background, then finances don't bother you as much. There is nothing at all wrong with that. It all depends on one's expectations.

- The women my father met were all professionals and expected more. The woman he married was a college graduate with a teenage daughter, but she needed someone to live off of and couldn't quite handle the world on her own. She lived with her parents for financial support, as she was divorced from her first husband. She took a liking to my dad, and he decided to date her. She was smart enough to see that he could manage okay, and it was the ticket she was looking for.

- Finances for most people will dictate life. It will dictate how we live life. Most working professionals will be okay with their choices and make the proper adjustments with their finances to be able to provide for their family.

Yes, as a working professional, we would all like to make a good living, and even become financially secure with solid investments. It does happen many times where working professionals are well off; they might not be rich, but they are well off. It also happens where working professionals are over-extended, so they search for another source of income. Many working professionals do something on the side to earn extra income. I always refer to my father in this last instance. He always lived above his means. He spent money on his girlfriends and went out often. He worked over the summer for a few extra dollars, teaching two classes each summer for extra money. He had a couple of other side jobs dealing with his profession as well. He taught at Fort Dix for a short time when the military wanted their higher-ranking officers to know proper English. I remember only one class that he taught there, which was kind of funny; he was a short guy, about 5'6", and he was teaching military brass. He had never served in the military, but he was teaching generals proper English, but he kept it professional. He also did book reviews for a couple of publishers. It didn't pay much, but he did it for a short time. He wasn't financially on his feet until he took early retirement. He took a buy-out from the college (though he would later admit it was a mistake to do so). The financial gain from taking the buy-out seemed too attractive for him and his wife, especially with the lifestyle they wanted, as they were both very good at spending money. When he was able to get his pension plus social security, he first paid off his unsecured debts – a first in his life. He moved (with his second wife) a few times. Why he kept on moving, I have no idea, but he at least had cleared his debts and was on a fixed income. He hoped his retirement would be enough to last all her remaining years. Whether that's true or not we will never know. His second wife and our family did not stay in touch after his death; he had never set that up for us, and we were not close.

3. Getting married for money

i.   This is terrible, but let's face it: people get married for money. It's nothing to be shocked by. A couple of really dumb situations I know of involve a guy who had some money. He was not rich by any means, but he had a bit of savings, so he wasn't suffering. He met a woman, she wanted to marry him, so they got married. After they spent his savings, she dumped him. I've actually seen this several times and just shake my head.

- My father didn't have any savings, as he always lived above his means, but he made a decent living as a college professor. One of his girlfriends actually moved in with him. All of us had long left the house, plus this was sometime after he had met the several women he could have settled down with. He continued to date. One woman was a blonde. We didn't know her, not until she called my house looking for his family – she wanted to give him a birthday party. When I did see him again, he said they were trying things out and living together. She had her own house, or was renting one, he had the good job in her opinion, and he had plenty of credit. I would later find out from his next girlfriend, who was much more level-headed than him, that the previous one, the blonde, basically furnished her house on his credit. I figured he wasn't using his head, not when it came to women, so this news proved my assumptions. Talking to him just a little bit about it, the thing he was surprised about was how she was allowed to charge well over his credit limit. She charged away, not caring about how much she was spending, and she had the credit line increased sizably. As soon has he found out, he had to cancel his cards. Back in those days, there wasn't any kind of instant notification, plus it was well before home computers. So he was notified only after he received his statements (which totally shocked him), and he was stuck holding this sizable debt. His new girlfriend at the time was a bit mad at how bad he managed his finances. He was a college English professor, with a PhD, but he could not manage his finances. She was very intelligent with a strong head. They really didn't date for all that long, which I thought was too bad, but she also had some higher expectations. She was strong-willed, and my father didn't have the finances or personality that would suit her.

ii. Someone who is well off wants to find a good partner as well. There is nothing wrong with a wealthy person wanting a spouse. A wealthy person just needs to be more careful. Hopefully, a wealthy person will pay attention to the other principles that are required for a real relationship. The last thing a wealthy person needs is a gold-digger. Being smart and being wealthy is good. To get wealthy after you meet your life partner is a plus. The rich and famous have a lifestyle that most of us will never experience. Yes, they too have families. Many believe they live in the clouds. They are simply on a different vibration than us commoners. There is nothing wrong with being wealthy. Most of us wish we were in that boat and living the lifestyle of our dreams. Some points to think about:

- The wealthy often don't trust common people, and they certainly won't associate with them. The wealthy person knows that the mindset is important. As the saying goes, your lifestyle will be reflective of your 5 closest friends.

Many people who have poor friends think they have to get rich friends to adjust their own mindset, and that is correct. If you think poor, you are poor. If you associate with rich, you will have a much better chance of success. Your mindset is what gives you ideas. Everything in life starts off with a thought. Then one must take that thought and put it into words, then deeds. Having the right positive thought and taking massive action helps people become successful. There are many books written on this subject, so I will not repeat it here. Your mindset is what starts you on your path to success.

- A smart, wealthy person will have little trouble finding a good partner. Some may not believe this, but there are plenty of good people out there. There are actually several people who would make a good spouse for any of us. Finding the right person is the difficult part. Many will find someone at work. A rich person will have more than enough people of interest to choose from. Some may disagree with that, but it comes down to expectation and recognizing a good situation when it's right in front of you. That could be a tough one to swallow. A rich person might have to move ego out of the way just a bit and understand that the right person for them is there. Lack of trust, or even lack of knowing what you want, can both be barriers.

- A corporate executive is a good example. Most rich corporate executives are business-minded individuals 24/7. It is all they think about. They do not have a balanced life. Working 12 to 18 hours a day, six and a half days a week is very normal. In the world of finance, business deals made late at night, on the weekends, and at 3 am on Monday morning are very common. Now many of them, or most of them, do have families, which makes it much easier to search for a spouse, but family comes second. They are business-minded first, and the spouse must understand that. That person will typically find someone in college, then have an "in" to a corporate job. The lifestyle is foreign to most of us, but very normal for that person and the reason for their success.

- The rich and famous are another matter. They love the spotlight. They crave the public life.

For them, that is the key to success. Many people want to get into the entertainment industry; they think fame and fortune are just waiting for them. Of course, talent is what separates those who want it from those who achieve that level of success. For the person looking for that type of success, you must focus on your talents. It takes hard work and dedication, with no guarantee. But those people are doing what they love. They are doing what is in their blood. A musician is not very good at factory work, just like a factory worker might have a hidden talent but might not be ready for an acting job.

- We all have our talents and are all capable of making a good living if we apply ourselves to that task. Dreaming big is good. Dreaming big without taking clear and decisive action to reach your goal is limiting.

iii. Everyone will have their reasons for how they approach life. Not everyone will think of the financial benefit that someone who is well-off could bring them. Always look for the other principles (ingredients) as well.

IN CONCLUSION

I have brought you what I believe are the most important aspects of a relationship. Of course, there are so many little nuances that go along with everyday life, but these four points are the main building blocks that every relationship needs.

- Personalities
- Mental Stimulation
- Sexual Satisfaction
- Financial Security

I will assure you, you will have a happy relationship if you pay attention to these four basic principles. While there are no guarantees in life, as people change through time, those of you who follow these principles will be much better off and live life with a good partner.

ABOUT THE AUTHOR

K.E. Martin is a purchase and contract manager in public housing for over a decade, and has had a two-decade long career in manufacturing. He holds an MBA.

His complicated marriage with his wife of over 20 years has probed him to introspect and explore the dimensions of long-lasting relationships. Years of observation and research have led K.E. Martin to pen down his first book, **Success or Failure in Your Relationship**. Here he shares the insights he has learned along the way and intends to assist people to help choose the right life partner and thrive in a strong and fulfilling marriage.

K.E. Martin is a father to two children and currently lives in New Jersey.

Made in the USA
Columbia, SC
14 November 2020

24516357R00046